How to Sparkle at
Counting to 10

Moira Wilson

Brilliant
PUBLICATIONS

We hope you and your class enjoy using this book. Other books in the series include:

To find out more details on any of our resources, please log onto our website: www.brilliantpublications.co.uk.

Published by Brilliant Publications
Unit 10, Sparrow Hall Farm, Edlesborough, Dunstable, Bedfordshire, LU6 2ES, UK

Sales and stock enquiries:
Tel: 01202 712910
Fax: 0845 1309300
E-mail: brilliant@bebc.co.uk
Website: www.brilliantpublications.co.uk

General information enquiries:
Tel: 01525 222292

The name Brilliant Publications and the logo are registered trademarks.

Written by Moira Wilson
Illustrated by Moira Wilson

Printed in the UK.
First published in 1998. Reprinted 2002 and 2010.
10   9   8   7   6   5   4   3

© Moira Wilson 1998
ISBN 978 1 897675 27 4

Contents

Introduction

This book contains a wealth of high interest activities and games which will enable children to develop a thorough understanding of numbers to 10. The activities are grouped into different mathematical concepts and each section is clearly marked in the contents list.

One-to-one matching, pages 6 to 9	These activities do not assume the ability to count. Instead, they focus on the use of one-to-one matching to compare equivalent groups of objects.
Cardinal number, pages 10 to 25	These pages deal with recognition of the number property of a set, the naming of numbers from 1 to 10 and the correct way to write the numbers and their associated words. Pages 20 to 25 offer valuable reinforcement activities.
Patterns in counting, pages 26 to 30	These pages require children to create patterns and repeat sequences.
More/fewer than, pages 31 to 34	The concept of inequality of number is dealt with on these pages. The word 'less' could be used if preferred in place of 'fewer'.
Ordinal numbers, page 35 to 42	These activities focus on the order and position of numbers 1 to 10. They encourage children to make connections between cardinal numbers, ordinal numbers and counting.
Reinforcement, page 43 to 48	An assortment of games and activities that will allow children to practise numerical skills and consolidate numerical concepts dealt with on the preceding pages.

Links to the National Curriculum

Close reference has been made to the National Curriculum in the writing of this book. The activities relate to the following programmes of study for Key Stage 1:

Pupils should be given opportunities to:

Number
2a   count orally up to 10, knowing the number names; count collections of objects, checking the total;
2b   read, write and order numbers, initially to 10;
3a   use repeating patterns to develop ideas of regularity and sequencing.

Using and applying mathematics
2b   select and use mathematical equipment and materials;
2d   organize and check their work;
3a   understand the language of number;
3c   discuss their work, responding to and asking mathematical questions;
4a   recognize simple patterns and relationships and make related predictions about them.

Successful linking of the activities to the programmes of study depends to some extent on the way they are presented to children and subsequent adult input. In the following section, there are suggestions as to how to present and use the ideas in the book.

How to use this book

The activities in this book can be used to complement any mathematics scheme that is being followed. It is not essential to use them in the order they appear in the book. Rather, the book can be 'dipped into' to give children support, practice or consolidation as and when the teacher feels it is necessary.

The text on each page has been kept to a minimum and, ideally, the teacher should discuss the instructions with the children as a group before asking them to embark on the task. It goes without saying that the activity pages should always be preceded by practical experiences to ensure the sound acquisition of mathematical concepts. For example:

Page 14
To introduce number 5, a variety of techniques could be used:

◆ form the numeral with Plasticine, clay or playdough;

◆ practise writing the numeral in a sand-filled tray;

◆ make 5 balls using Plasticine, clay or playdough;

◆ make sets of 5 objects, encouraging the children to choose counting equipment and set rings found in most infant classrooms;

◆ make towers with 5 interlocking cubes, asking each child to choose a different colour;

◆ thread beads on to laces in groups of 5;

◆ encourage the use of mathematical language by asking questions such as, 'How many more balls of Plasticine do you need to make 5?'

◆ teach number rhymes and songs such as 'Five fat sausages' and 'Five little ducks went swimming one day'.

When the child is involved in completing the page, a teacher/adult can encourage deeper mathematical thinking by asking leading questions such as:

◆ Why haven't you drawn a ring round this set?

◆ Why does this set need a ring?

◆ Are there more snails than ducks?

◆ How many sets of 5 did you draw a ring round?

When completed and dated, the pages can be stored in the children's mathematical folders creating a useful record of work covered.

The games on pages 43, 47 and 48 will last longer if the photocopied sheets are stuck to pieces of card and laminated. Store the laminated game boards in plastic wallets with the necessary props.

Hungry birds

Draw a line from each bird to a snail.

Draw a line from each bird to a worm.

Missing objects

Draw a tail on each mouse.

Draw some ice-cream in each cone.

Draw a cherry on each cake.

In the garden

Draw a line from each caterpillar to a leaf.

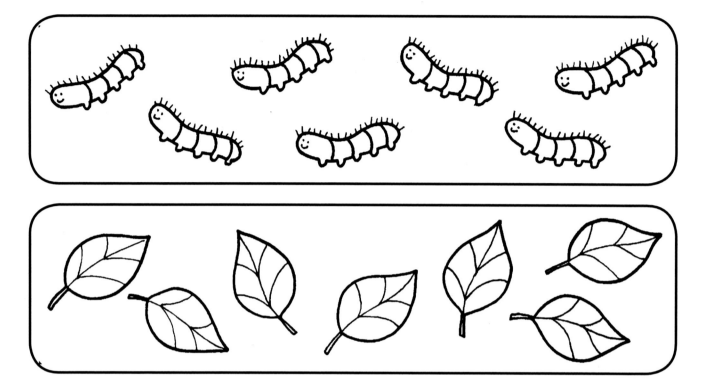

Draw a line from each butterfly to a flower.

More missing objects

Draw a straw in each glass.

Draw a flower in each vase.

Draw an egg in each egg-cup.

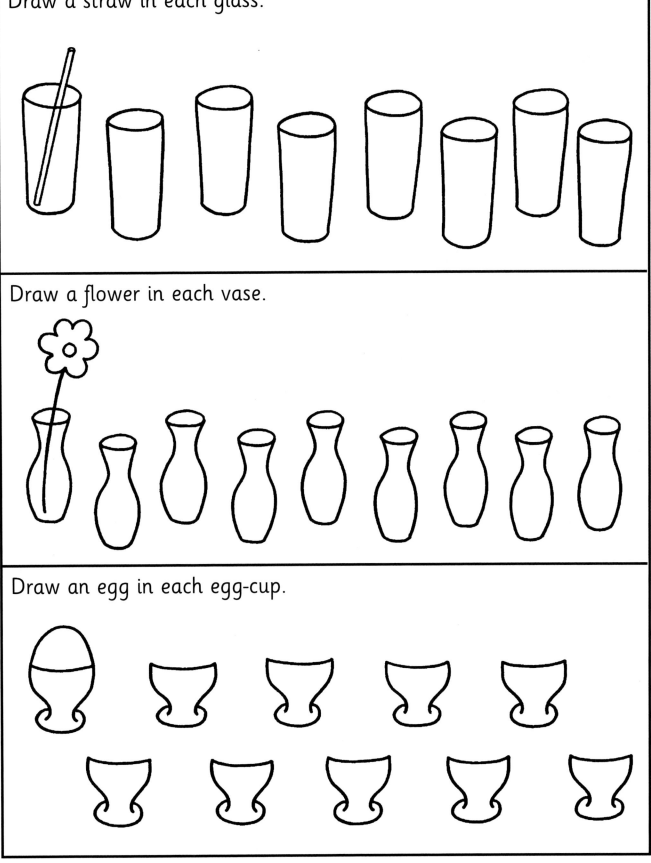

Counting to 1

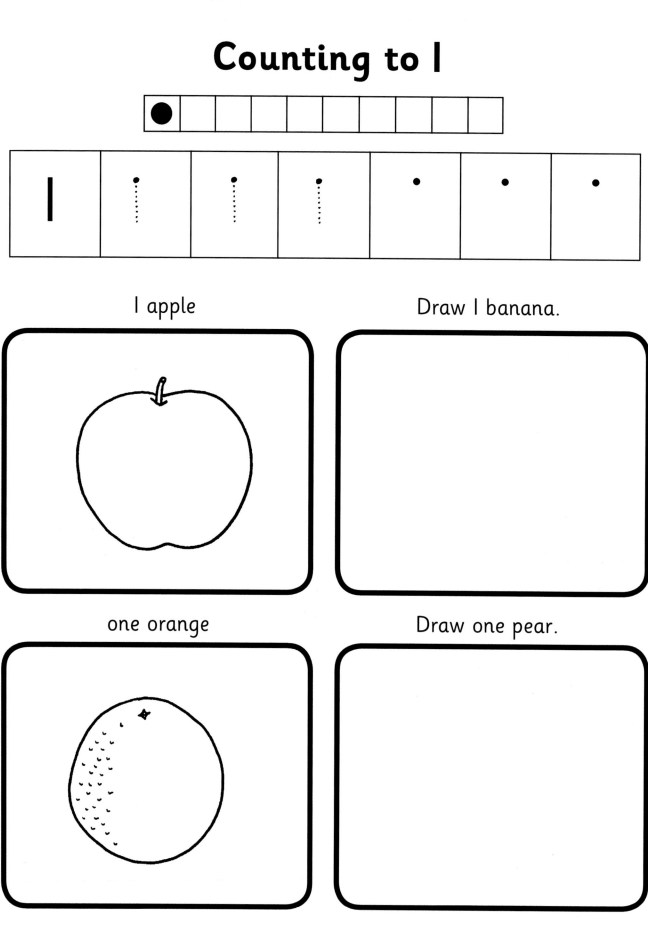

1 apple

Draw 1 banana.

one orange

Draw one pear.

one

Counting to 2

| 2 | 2 | 2 | 2 | • | • | • |

2 horses

Draw 2 dogs.

two sheep

Draw two cats.

| two | two | • |

Counting to 3

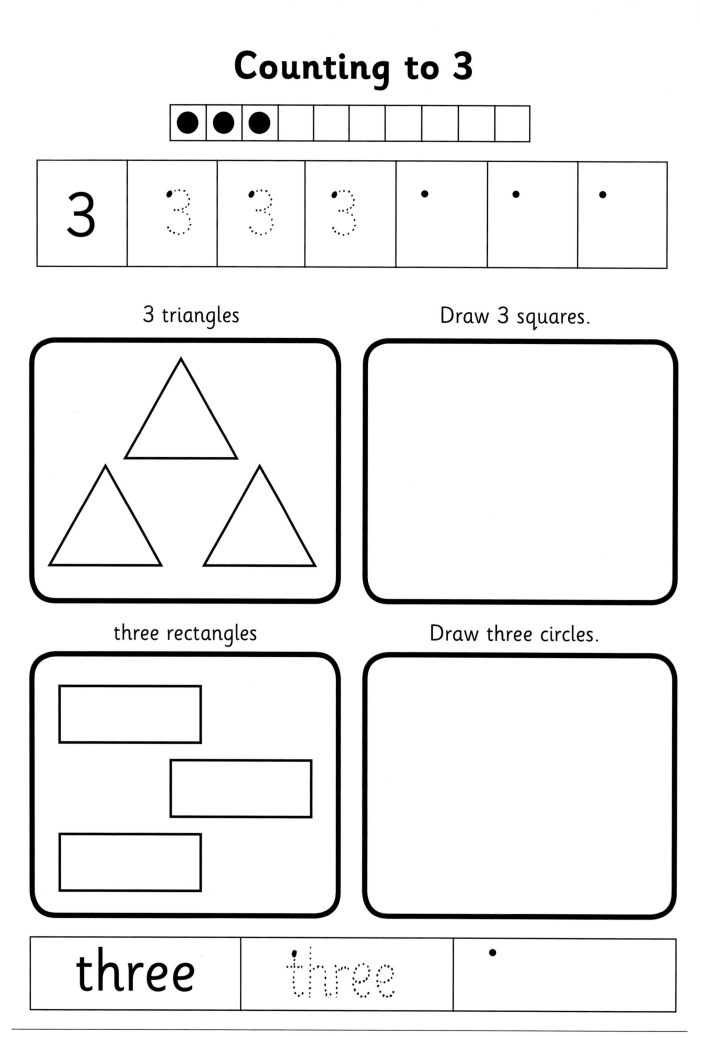

3 triangles

Draw 3 squares.

three rectangles

Draw three circles.

three   three

Counting to 4

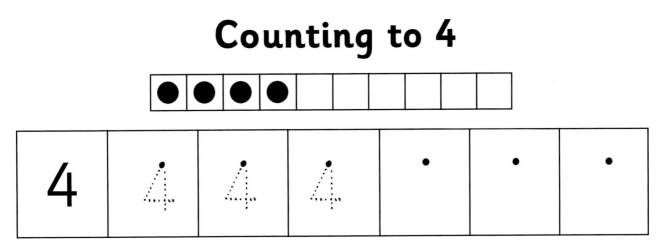

Draw a ring round the sets of 4 and colour the objects.

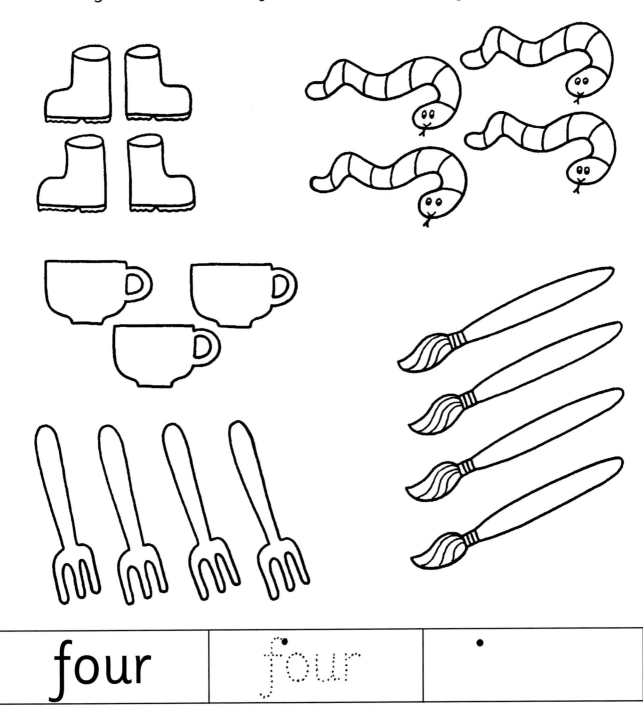

four   four

Counting to 5

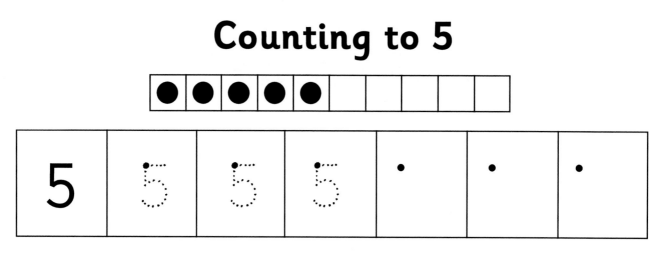

Draw a ring round the sets of 5 and colour the objects.

five	five	.

Counting to 6

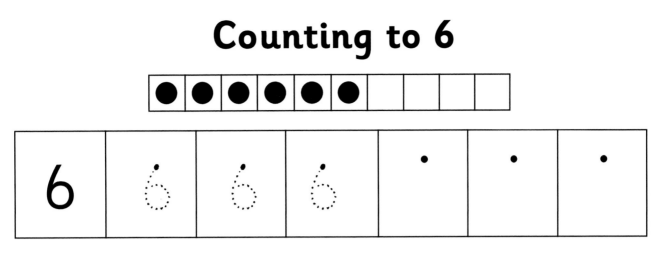

6   6   6   6

Draw a ring round the sets of 6 and colour the objects.

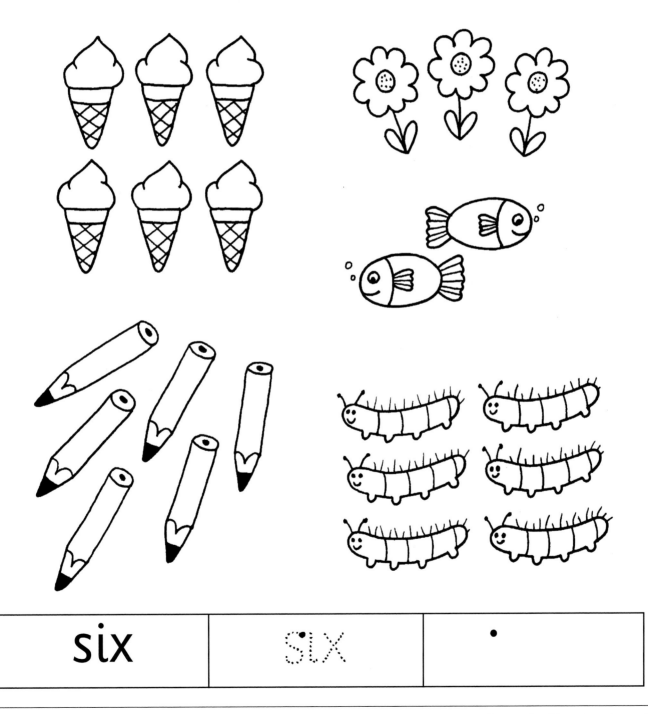

six	six	

Counting to 7

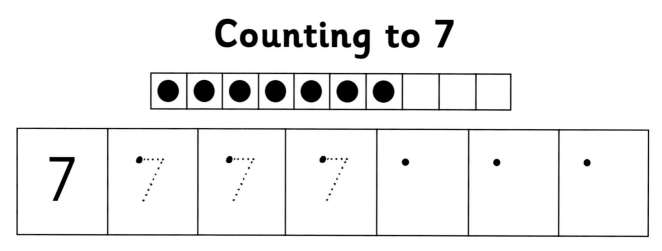

Draw a ring round the sets of 7 and colour the objects.

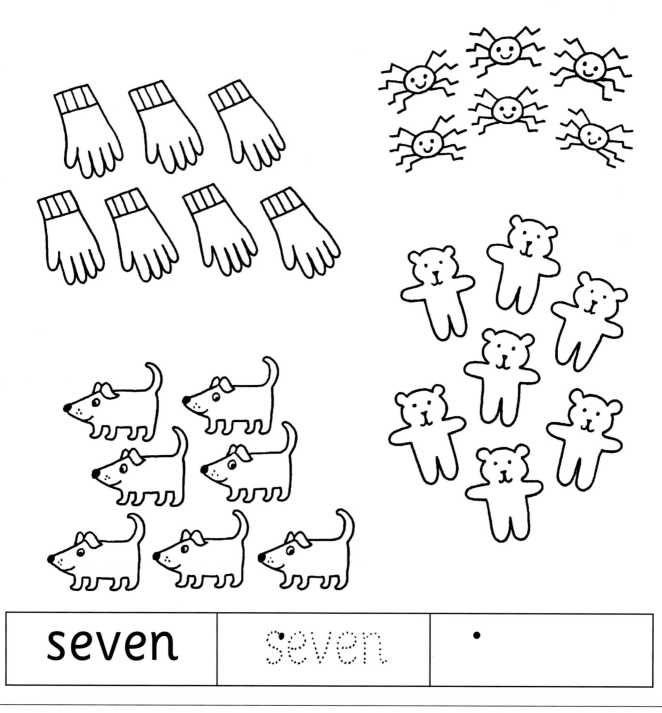

| seven | seven | . |

Counting to 8

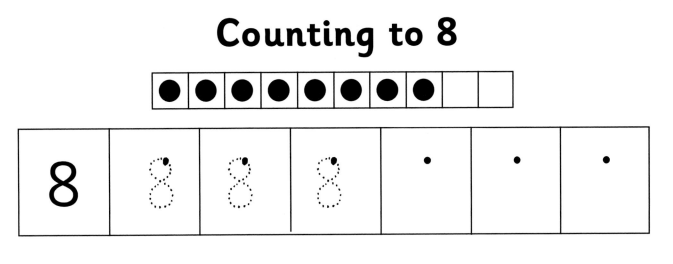

8   8   8   8

Colour the set of 8 objects.

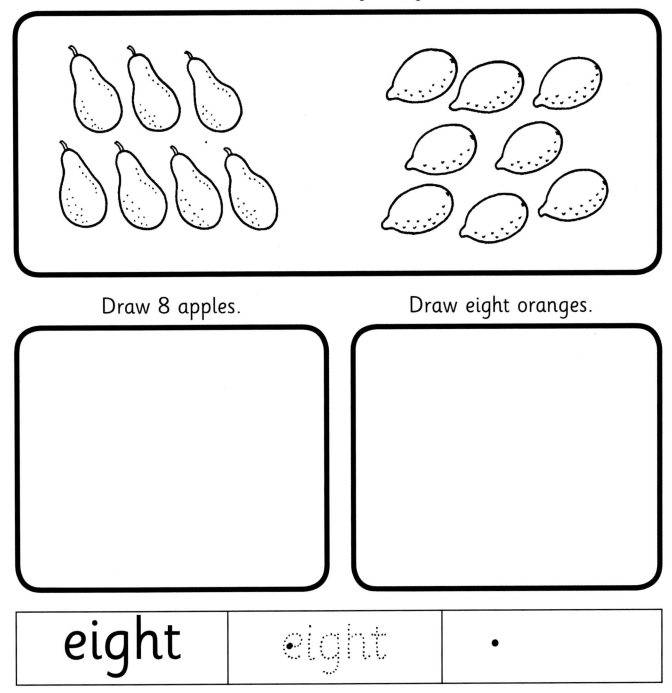

Draw 8 apples.

Draw eight oranges.

eight   eight

Counting to 9

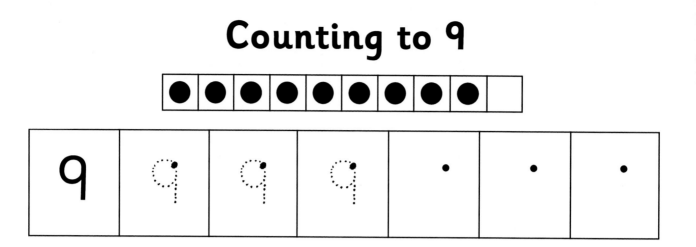

9 9 9 9 • • •

Colour the set of 9 objects.

Draw 9 sweets.

Draw nine lollipops.

nine   nine   •

Counting to 10

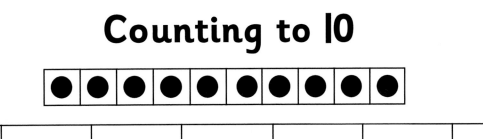

10	10	10	10	··	··	··

Colour the set of 10 objects.

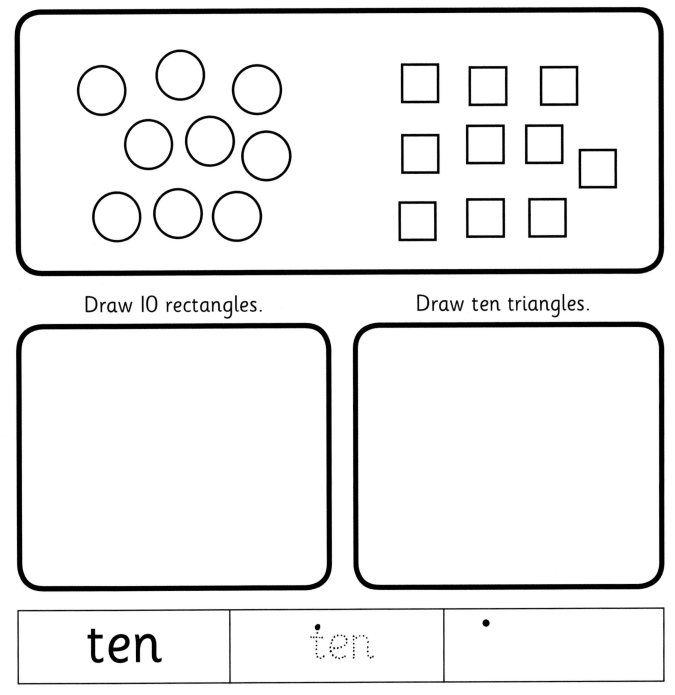

Draw 10 rectangles.

Draw ten triangles.

ten	ten	·

Spotty ladybirds

Draw the correct number of spots for each ladybird.

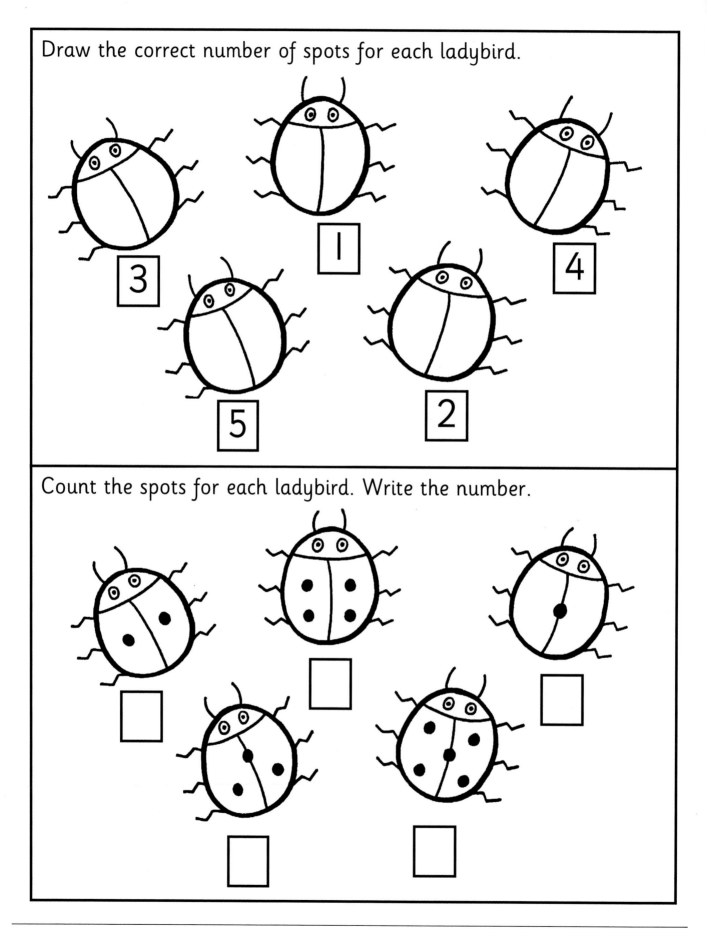

Count the spots for each ladybird. Write the number.

Once I caught a fish alive 1 – 5

1 one	2 two	3 three	4 four	5 five

Write the numbers and words.

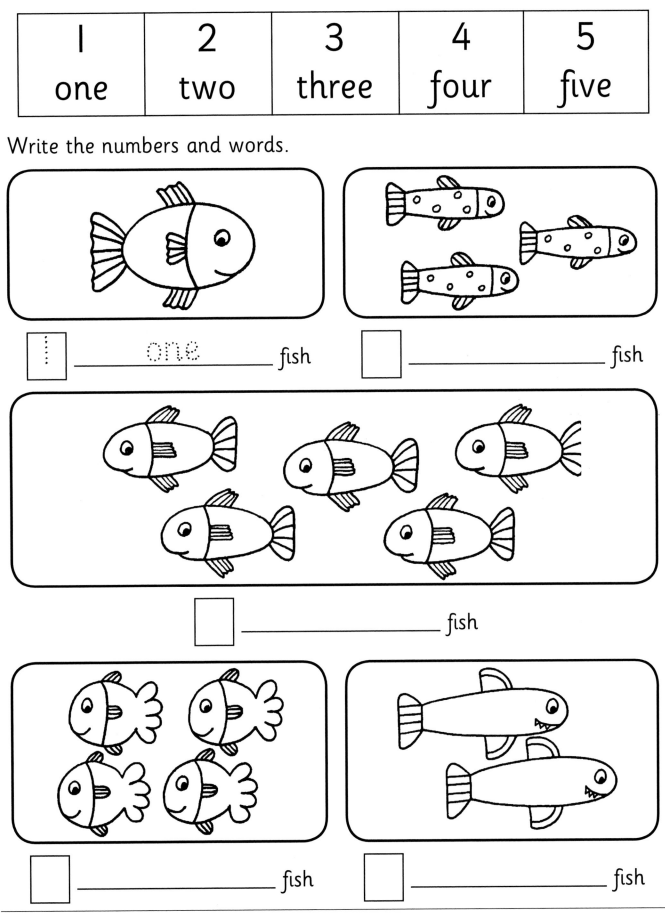

1 ....one........ fish

☐ _____ fish

☐ _____ fish

☐ _____ fish

☐ _____ fish

Domino match 1 – 5

Draw lines from each domino to the correct number and word.

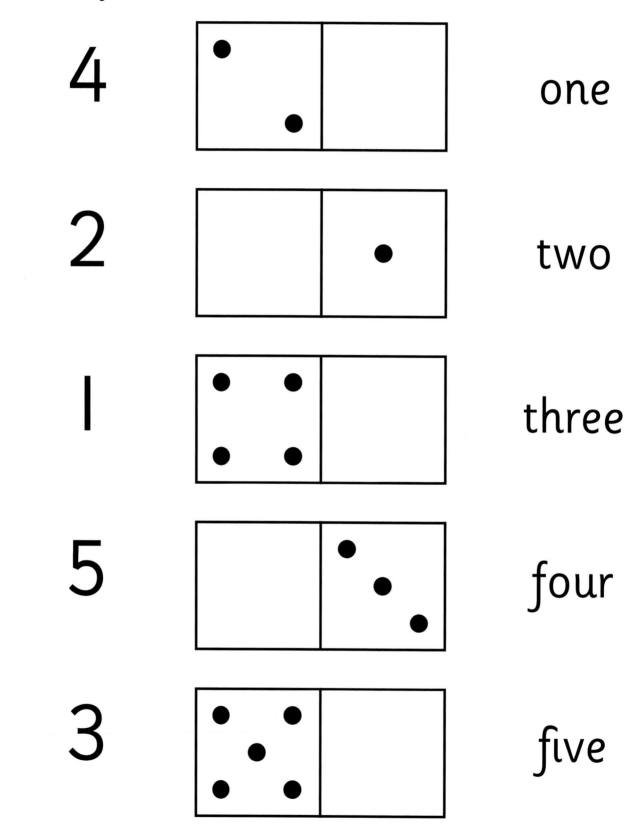

4   one

2   two

1   three

5   four

3   five

Jumping frogs

Draw the jumps and write the numbers in the stones.
Write the total number of jumps in the box.

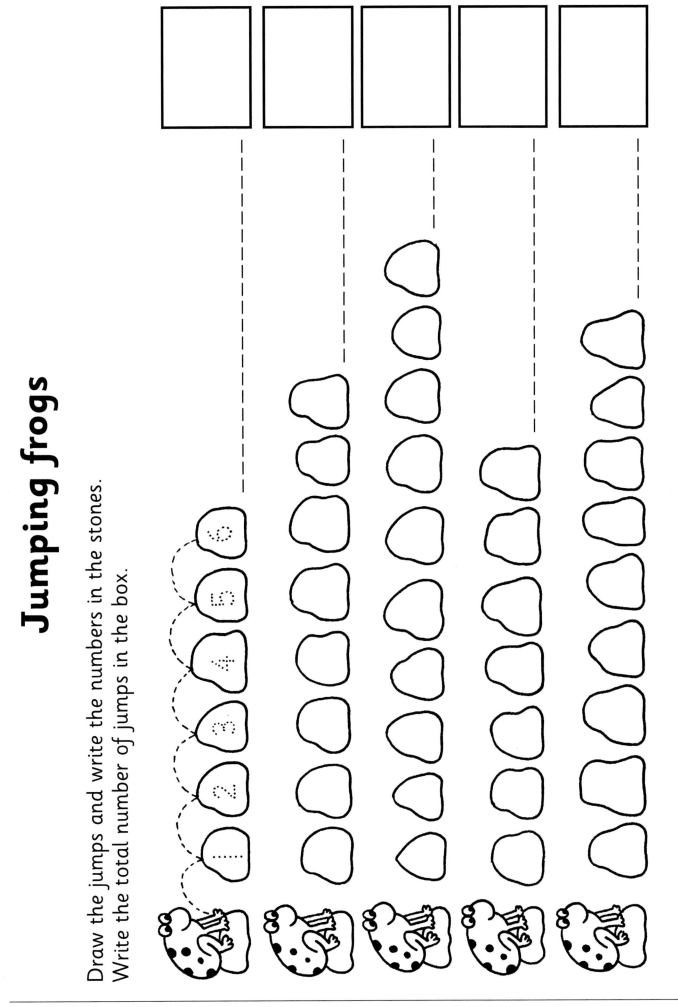

Once I caught a fish alive 6 – 10

6	7	8	9	10
six	seven	eight	nine	ten

Write the numbers and words.

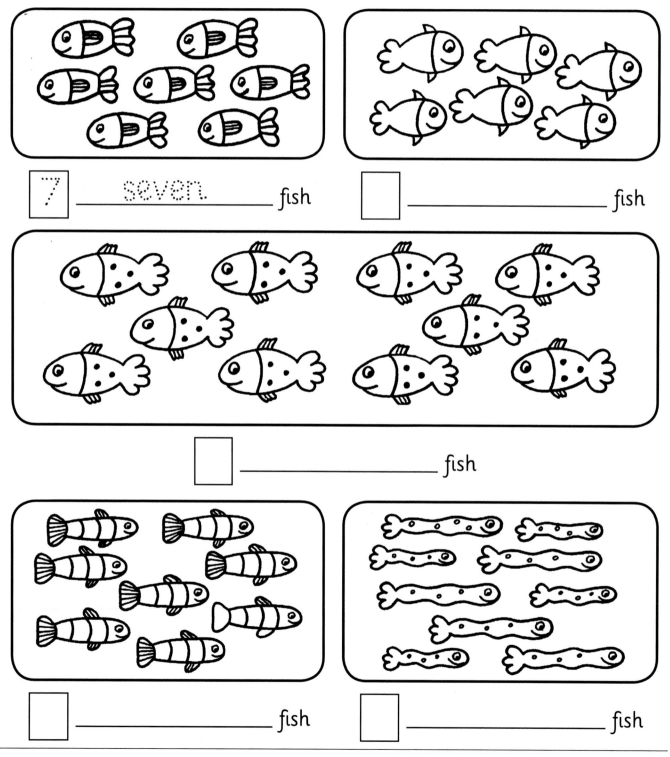

7 _seven_ _____ fish

☐ _____ fish

☐ _____ fish

☐ _____ fish

☐ _____ fish

Domino match 6 – 10

Draw lines from each domino to the correct number and word.

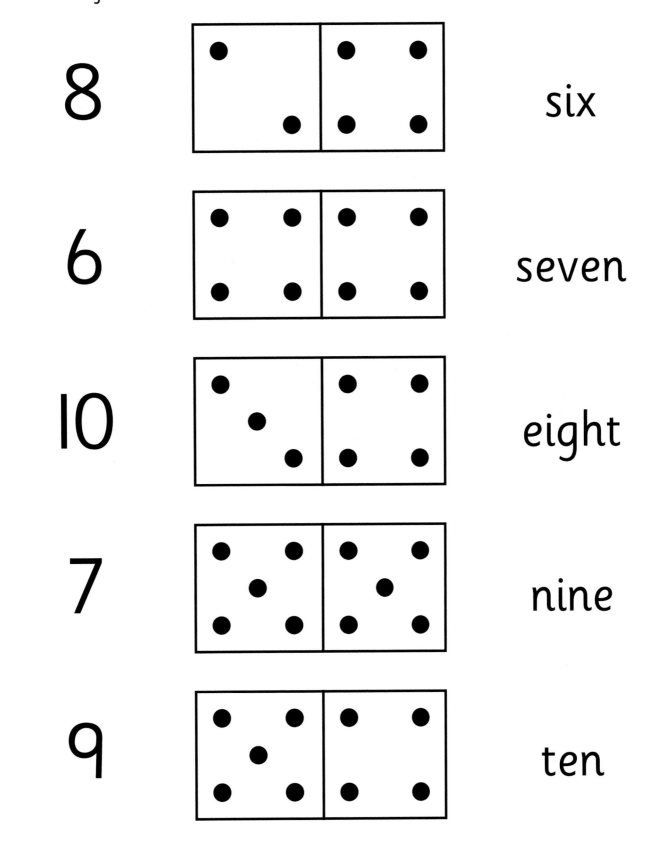

8   six

6   seven

10   eight

7   nine

9   ten

Spotty snakes

Continue the spotty patterns.

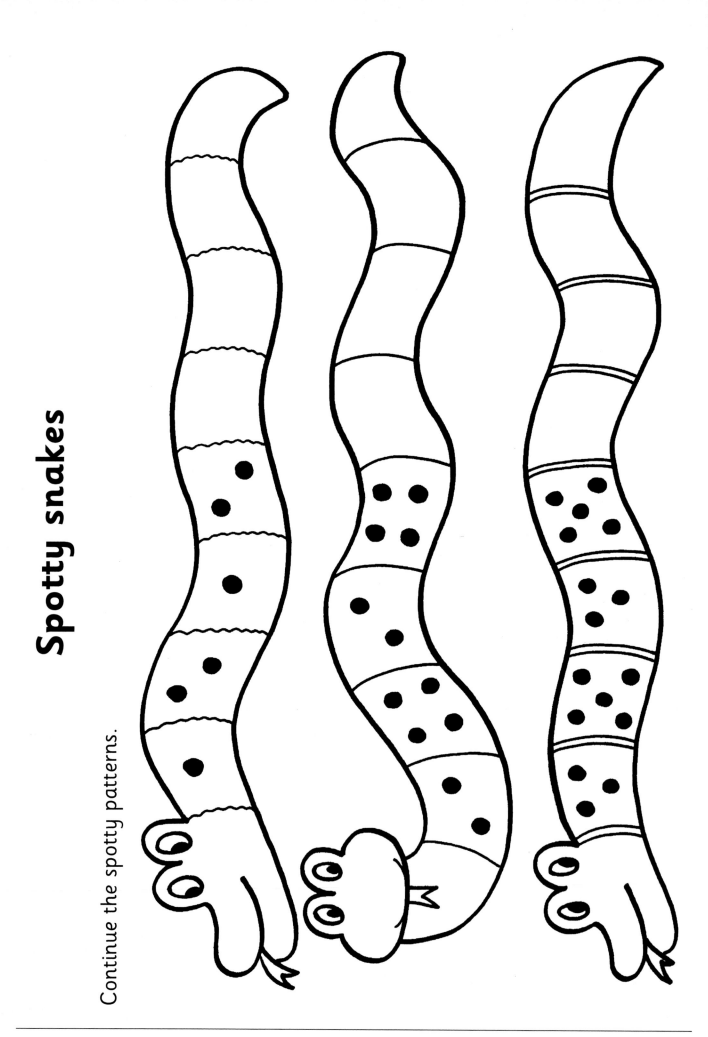

Flower patterns

Draw the missing petals and leaves and write the numbers.

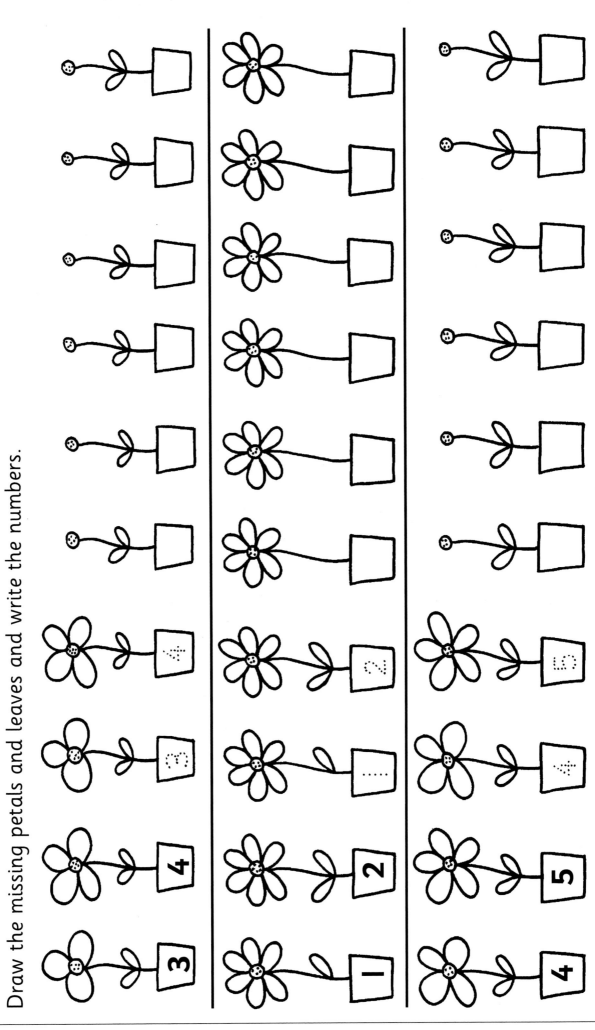

Square patterns

Colour 5 squares in each box. Use one colour only.

Make each pattern different.

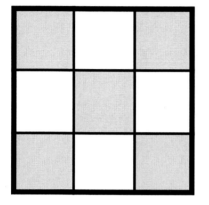 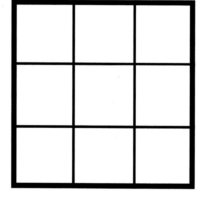 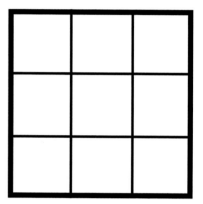

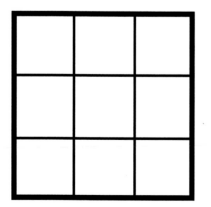 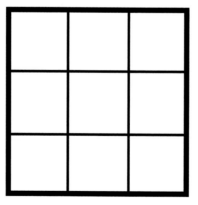 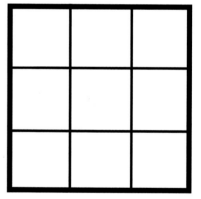

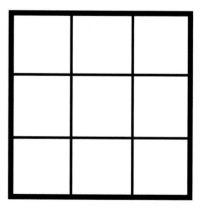

Clever seals

Continue the ball patterns.

Flying kites

Draw the spots on the kites and write the numbers.

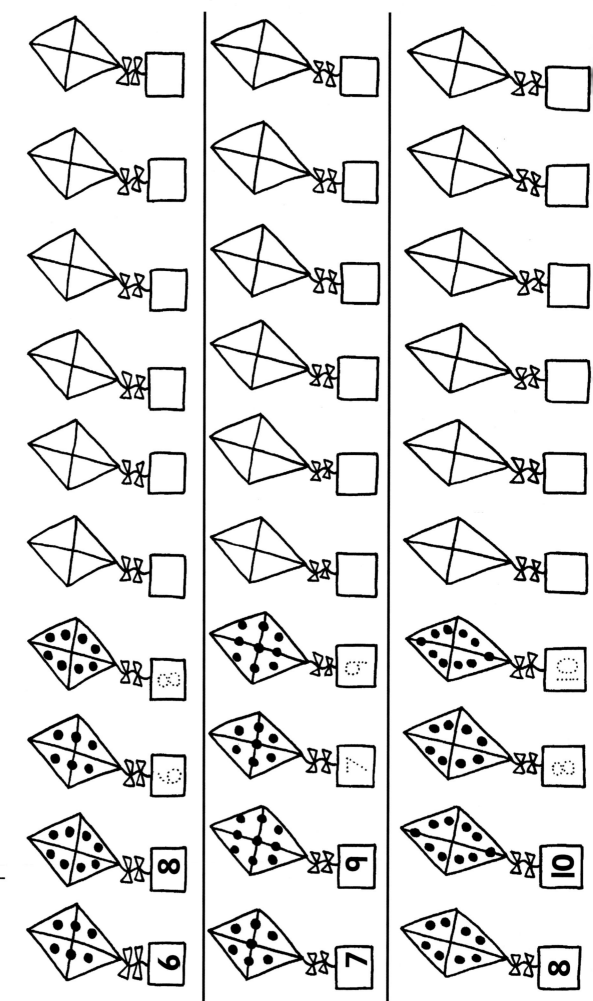

Egg count

If a duck has more than 2 eggs, colour it yellow.

If a duck has fewer than 2 eggs, colour it brown.

Flower count

If a vase holds more than 3 flowers, colour it yellow.

If a vase holds fewer than 3 flowers, colour it red.

Slithering snakes

If a snake has more than 6 black stripes, colour it red and green.

If a snake has fewer than 6 black stripes, colour it blue and yellow.

Munching monsters

If a monster has more than 7 spots, colour it blue.

If a monster has fewer than 7 spots, colour it green.

Racing cars

Colour the cars. Cut them out and stick them in numerical order.

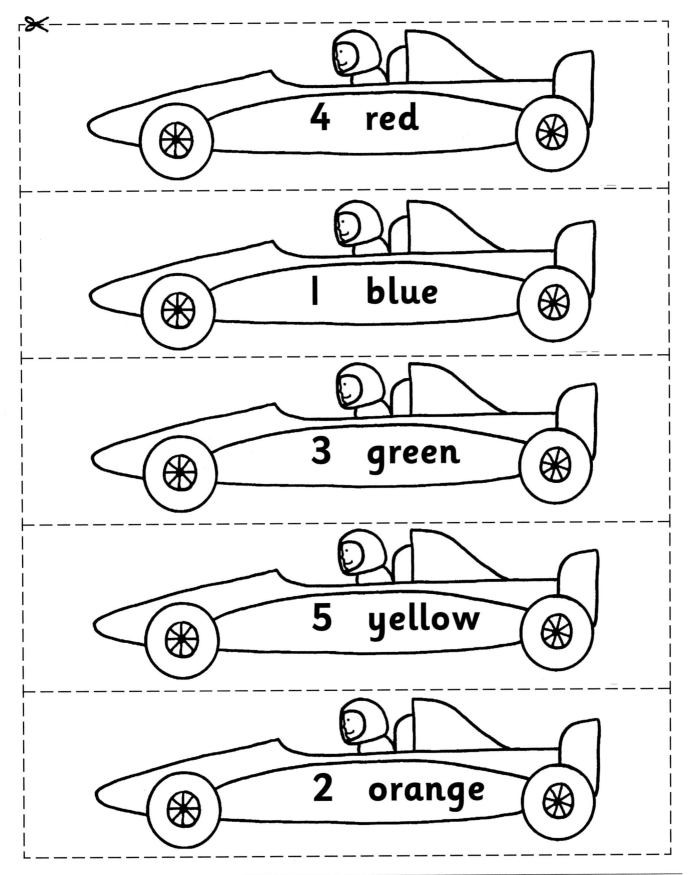

Racing yachts

Colour the yachts. Cut them out and stick them in numerical order.

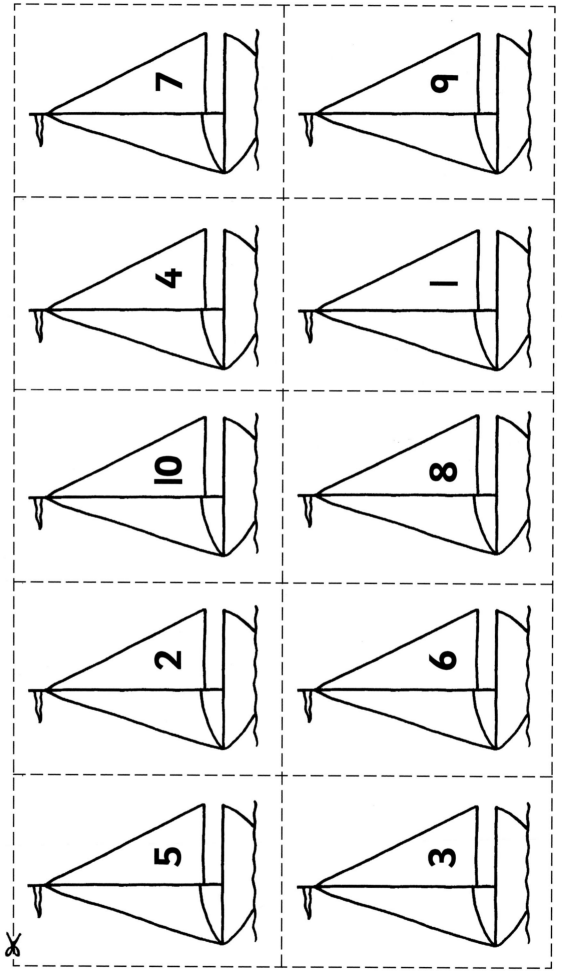

Musical dots

Join the dots in order.

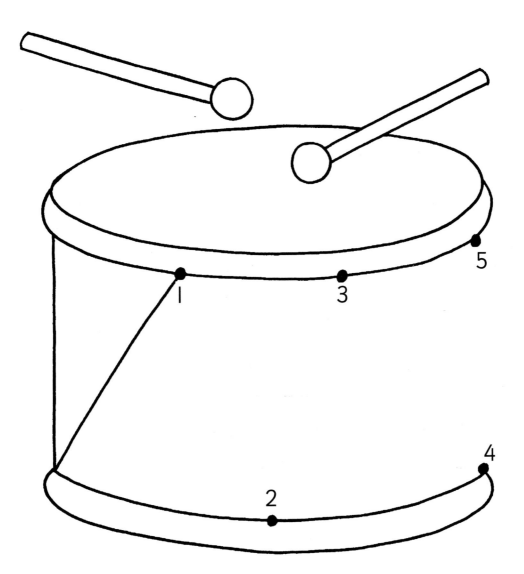

The numbers in the box are jumbled up.
Write them in order on the line below.

2	5	3	I	4

_____

Monster dots

Join the dots in order.

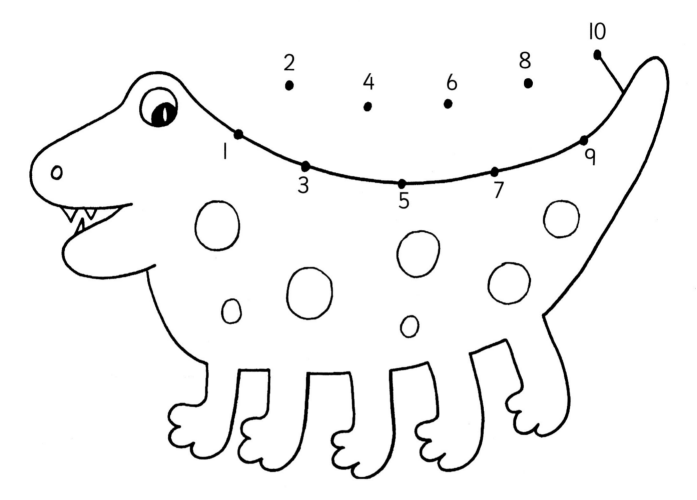

The numbers in the box are jumbled up.
Write them in order on the line below.

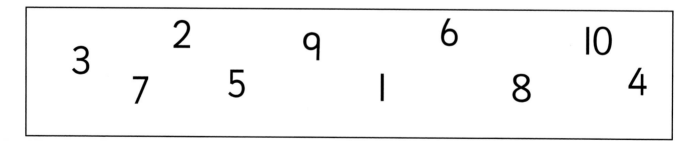

_____

Crawling caterpillars

Write the missing numbers.

Count backwards and write the missing numbers.

Snakes and ladders

Write the missing numbers.

The dog show 1 – 5

Cut the dogs out and stick them in order.

Cut out the rosettes. Give one to each dog.

The dog show 6 – 10

Cut the dogs out and stick them in order.

Cut out the rosettes. Give one to each dog.

eighth

sixth

ninth

seventh

tenth

6th   7th   8th   9th   10th

The apple tree game

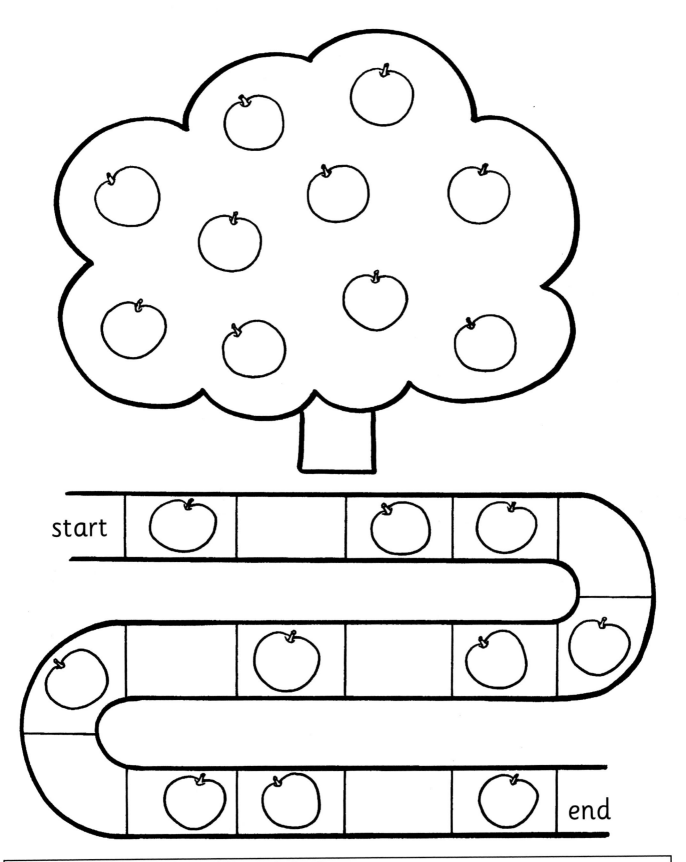

start

end

Equipment: a die, red counters for one child, green for the other.
The children take it in turns to throw the die, moving along the correct number of spaces. If they land on a picture of an apple, they have to cover one of the apples on the tree with a counter. When they have both reached the end, they count their 'apples' on the tree. The child with the most apples is the winner.

Dotty dice game, 1

You need 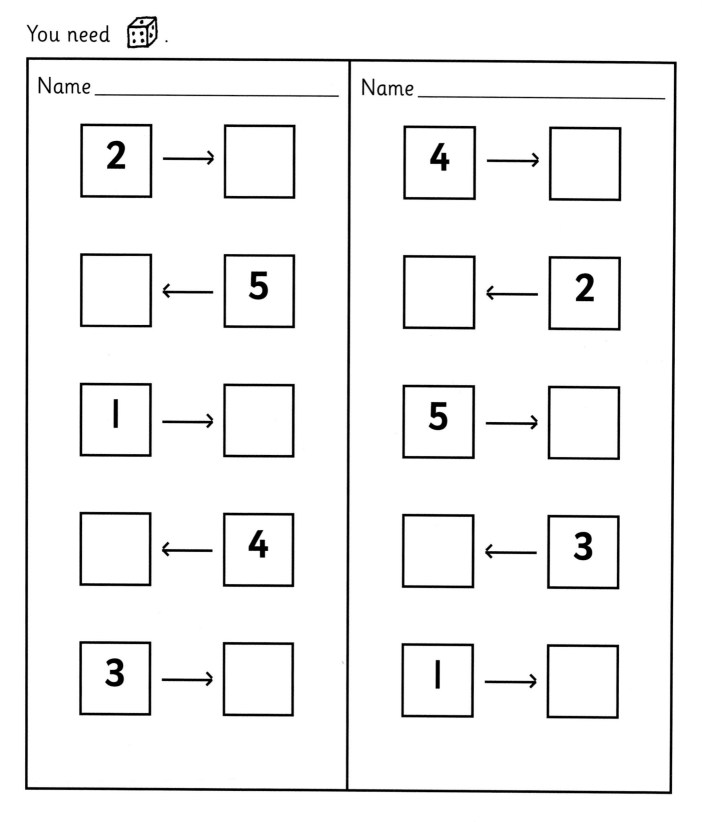 .

Name _____   Name _____

| 2 | → | ☐ | | 4 | → | ☐ |

| ☐ | ← | 5 | | ☐ | ← | 2 |

| 1 | → | ☐ | | 5 | → | ☐ |

| ☐ | ← | 4 | | ☐ | ← | 3 |

| 3 | → | ☐ | | 1 | → | ☐ |

_____ is the winner.

Equipment: a die with dots.
The children take it in turns to throw the die. Whatever number is thrown, the child has to identify the corresponding numeral on the sheet and draw the correct number of dots in the box alongside. If a 6 or a repeat number is thrown, then play reverts to the other child. The first child to complete his/her column is the winner.

Dotty dice game, 2

You need 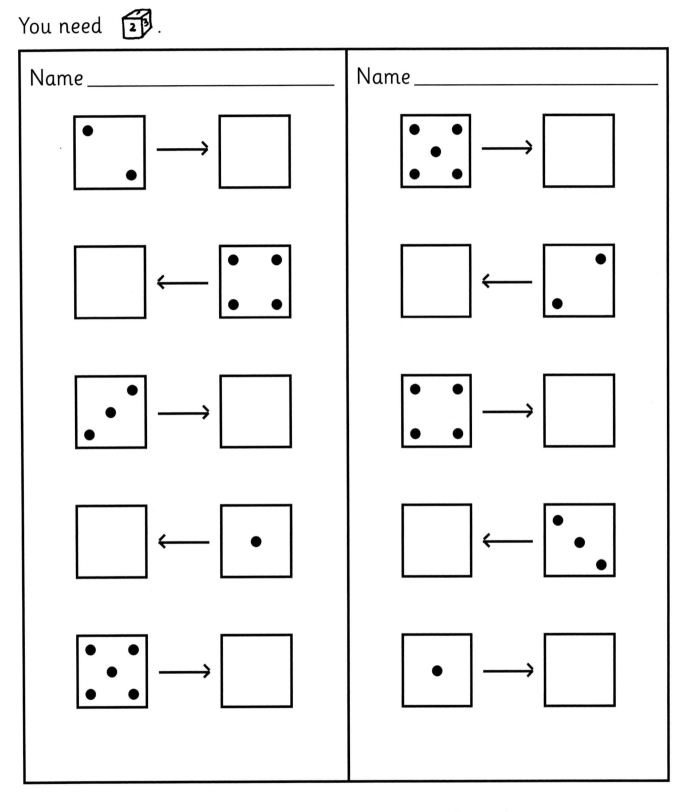.

Name _____   Name _____

_____ is the winner.

Equipment: a die with numbers.
The children take it in turns to throw the die. Whatever number is thrown, the child has to identify the corresponding dots on the sheet and write the correct numeral in the box alongside. If a 6 or a repeat number is thrown, then play reverts to the other child.
The first child to complete his/her column is the winner.

Rocket race

Name_____   Name_____

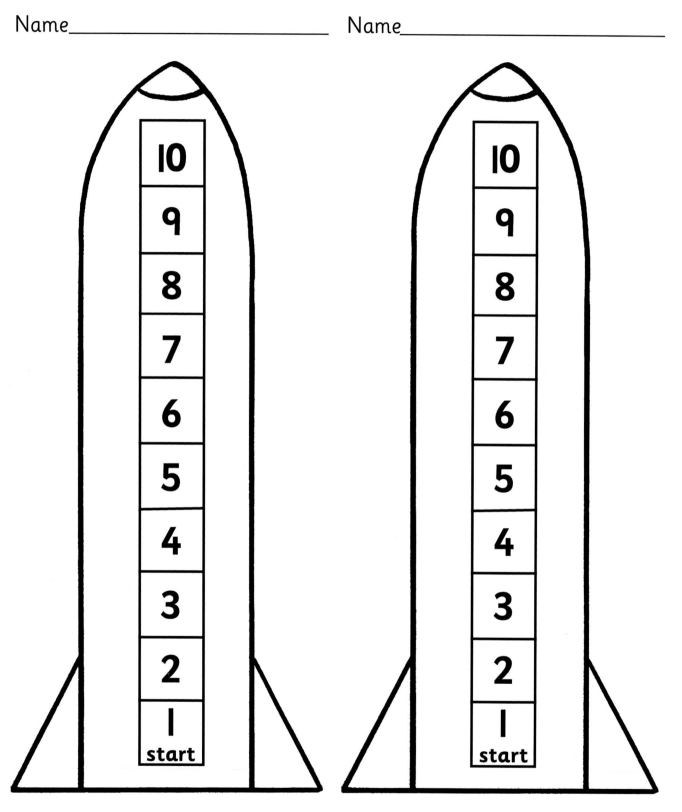

_____ is the winner.

Equipment: a die and 2 counters.
The children take it in turns to throw the die, moving up their respective rockets accordingly. The first child to reach the top is the winner but the final throw must be accurate to count as a valid throw. For example, a child on number 8 would need to throw a 2 to reach the top.

Treasure island

Equipment: a die and 2 counters.
The children take it in turns to throw the die, moving along the stepping stones accordingly. If they land on a stone near a shark, they have to go back to the start and resume their journey on the next throw. The first child to reach the treasure is the winner.

Number jigsaw

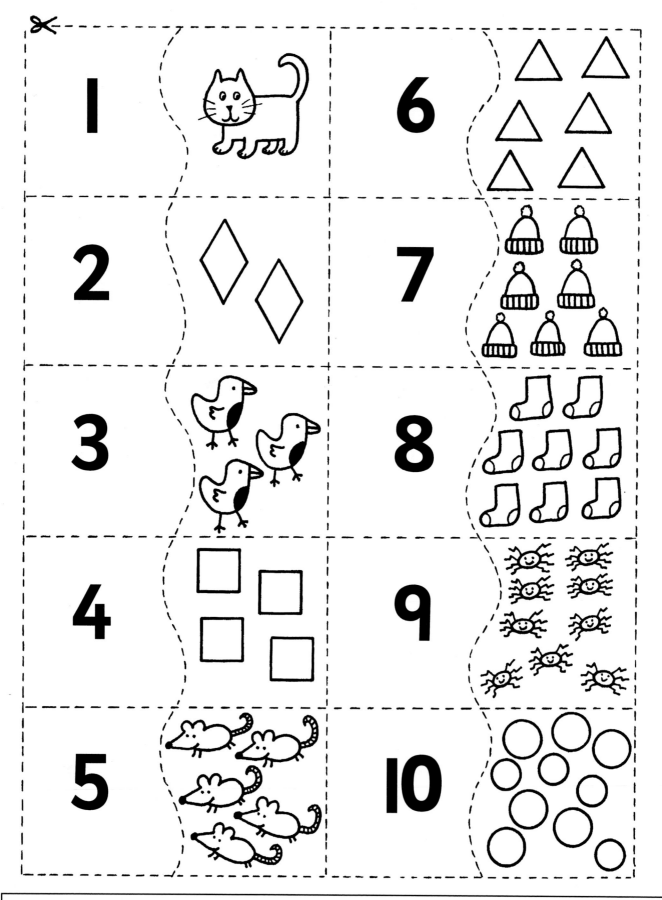

The children can colour the pictures before sticking the whole page on to card. Cut carefully along the broken lines and then try to piece the jigsaw back together again.